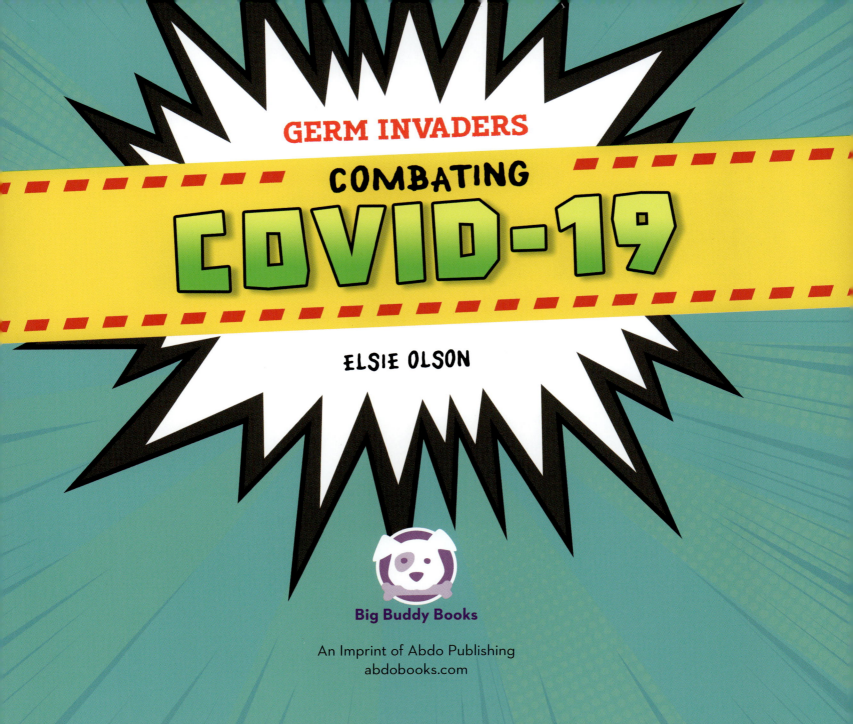

GERM INVADERS
COMBATING COVID-19

ELSIE OLSON

Big Buddy Books

An Imprint of Abdo Publishing
abdobooks.com

abdobooks.com

Published by Abdo Publishing, a division of ABDO, PO Box 398166, Minneapolis, Minnesota 55439. Copyright © 2021 by Abdo Consulting Group, Inc. International copyrights reserved in all countries. No part of this book may be reproduced in any form without written permission from the publisher. Big Buddy Books™ is a trademark and logo of Abdo Publishing.

Printed in the United States of America, North Mankato, Minnesota
102020
012021

Design: Sarah DeYoung, Mighty Media, Inc.
Production: Mighty Media, Inc.
Editor: Rebecca Felix

Cover Photographs: Alissa Eckert, MSMI, Dan Higgins, MAMS/Centers for Disease Control and Prevention (virus); Shutterstock (doctor in cape)
Interior Photographs: AP Images, p. 11; Shutterstock, pp. 4–9, 12–29
Design Elements: Shutterstock (all)

Library of Congress Control Number: 2020940269

Publisher's Cataloging-in-Publication Data
Names: Olson, Elsie, author.
Title: Combating COVID-19 / by Elsie Olson
Description: Minneapolis, Minnesota : Abdo Publishing, 2021 | Series: Germ invaders | Includes online resources and index
Identifiers: ISBN 9781532194221 (lib. bdg.) | ISBN 9781098213589 (ebook)
Subjects: LCSH: COVID-19 (Disease)--Juvenile literature. | Health behavior--Juvenile literature. | Immunology--Juvenile literature. | Health behavior--Juvenile literature. | Hygiene--Juvenile literature | Science--Experiments--Juvenile literature. | Viruses--Juvenile literature.
Classification: DDC 616.079--dc23

CONTENTS

Your Amazing Body 4
When COVID-19 Attacks 6
Coronavirus 101 8
COVID-19 Is Born 10
An Infection Spreads 14
The World Reacts 16
Social Distancing 18
Do You Have COVID-19? 20
Treating COVID-19 22
At the Hospital 24
What's Next? 26
Preventing COVID-19 28
Glossary 30
Online Resources 31
Index 32

YOUR AMAZING BODY

You are amazing! So is your body. Most of the time your body works just fine. But sometimes germs **invade** it. Germs can make you sick. In late 2019, a germ called SARS-CoV-2 swept the globe. It caused the **disease** COVID-19. Within months, millions of people were **infected**.

People tried to control the spread of COVID-19. Experts said wearing masks and staying home were the best ways to do this.

GET TO KNOW GERMS

Germs are tiny **organisms**. They can live inside people, plants, and animals. There are four main types of germs.

VIRUSES

Viruses are parasitic. This means they cannot survive on their own. They require a host cell to reproduce.

BACTERIA

Bacteria are single-celled creatures. They can survive on their own or inside another living organism.

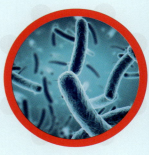

PROTOZOA

Protozoa are single-celled creatures. Some can survive on their own. Others are parasitic.

FUNGI

Fungi are plant-like organisms. They get their food from people, plants, and animals.

WHEN COVID-19 ATTACKS

The SARS-CoV-2 virus is microscopic. This means it is so small it cannot be **detected** by the human eye. But this tiny germ can create big trouble if it **invades** your body.

INVASION

A person near you sick with COVID-19 coughs, sneezes, or talks. Their germs enter the air. You breathe in the virus.

FINDING A HOST

The virus attaches to a host cell inside your body.

REPLICATION

The virus **releases** its **genetic** material into the host cell. It orders the cell to make copies. One virus **particle** can create thousands of copies.

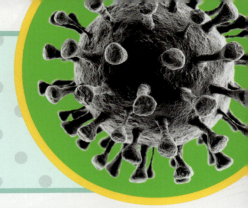

SPREADING

The virus copies spread throughout the body. They find new host cells. They continue to make copies. You release virus particles into the air when you cough, sneeze, and talk. Now the virus can **infect** others.

FIGHTING BACK

Your immune system **detects** and fights the virus.
- White blood cells attack the virus.
- Your body temperature may increase, causing a fever. This helps kill the virus.

CORONAVIRUS 101

SARS-CoV-2 is a type of **coronavirus**. These viruses cause **respiratory** illness in humans. Scientists have discovered many coronaviruses. And you've probably had one before! These viruses often cause common colds.

SARS-CoV-2 is novel. That means it has never been **detected** in humans before.

Corona means "crown" in Latin. Spikes cover coronavirus germs. Some people think it looks like the germs have crowns.

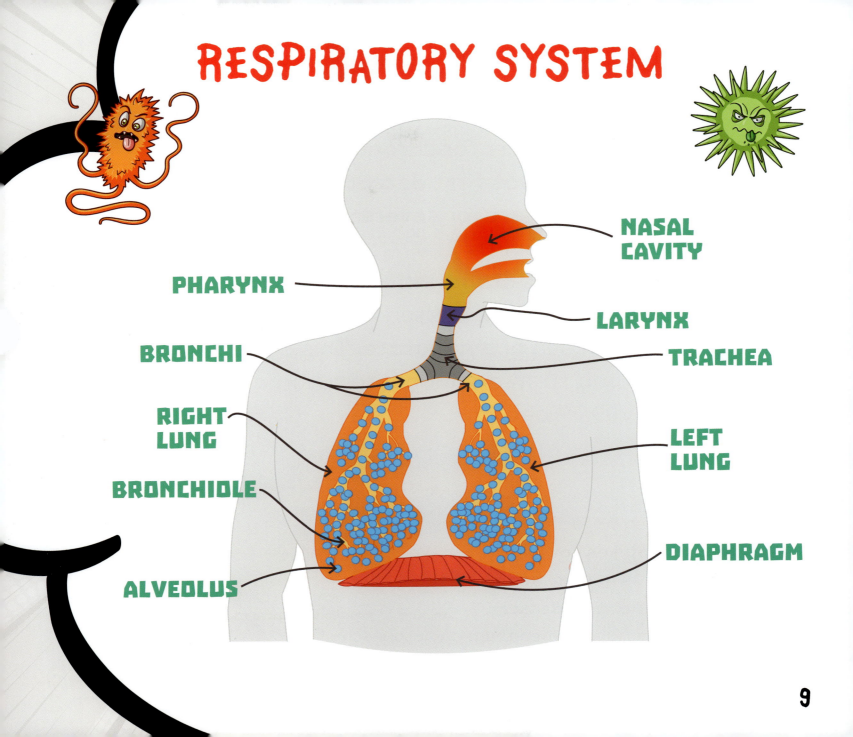

COVID-19 IS BORN

COVID-19 is short for **coronavirus disease** 2019. COVID-19 was first **detected** in late 2019. *SARS-CoV-2* is short for **severe** acute **respiratory** syndrome coronavirus 2.

Similar viruses are found in some animals. But most viruses can't be passed between **species**. However, viruses often **mutate**. This can allow the virus to jump from an animal to a human. This is how COVID-19 began.

SCIENCE BREAKTHROUGH

Chinese scientists **decoded** SARS-CoV-2's **genetic** information. This helped them and other scientists around the world study the virus.

From 2002 to 2003, a coronavirus called SARS-CoV sickened more than 8,000 people in 26 countries.

Scientists aren't sure exactly how SARS-CoV-2 jumped from animals to humans. The virus most likely **originated** in bats. From there it may have spread to another animal and then to humans.

The first reported cases of COVID-19 were in Wuhan, China. In December 2019, China reported flu-like **infections** in the city. In January 2020, the country discovered the infections were from a novel **coronavirus**.

Bats can have coronaviruses without becoming sick. They have a natural immunity to these viruses.

Wet markets sell meat, fish, produce, and sometimes live animals. Many early cases of COVID-19 were traced to a wet market in China.

AN INFECTION SPREADS

SARS-CoV-2 spread quickly. Within a few months, the virus had spread to many countries and **infected** millions of people. Hundreds of thousands of people died.

Governments and healthcare experts struggled to prepare for and battle COVID-19. Many countries, including the US, lacked enough supplies to **detect** and treat the virus.

Medical experts believe COVID-19 is deadlier than influenza.

#StayAtHome

As the number of COVID-19 cases rose, healthcare workers worldwide used social media to ask people to stay home. They hoped this would help stop or slow the virus's spread.

THE WORLD REACTS

On March 11, 2020, the World Health Organization (WHO) declared COVID-19 a **pandemic**. By then, the **disease** had spread to 114 countries. More than 4,000 people had died.

Health experts hoped to slow the spread while they worked to find a cure. But many countries had limited tests for the virus. This made it hard to know who had it and who didn't. And experts said even people not showing **symptoms** could have COVID-19 and be spreading it to others.

COVID-19 TIMELINE

DECEMBER 2019: China reports a cluster of flu-like **infections** in Wuhan.

JANUARY 11: China reports its first death from the virus.

FEBRUARY 11: The WHO names the novel coronavirus **disease** COVID-19.

MARCH 26: The number of US COVID-19 cases is greater than in any other country.

JANUARY 7, 2020: China reports that the infections are from a novel **coronavirus**.

JANUARY 21: The first US case of the virus is confirmed.

MARCH 11: Following outbreaks in several countries, the WHO declares COVID-19 a **pandemic**.

SEPTEMBER 29: The number of COVID-19 deaths worldwide passes one million. The pandemic continues.

SOCIAL DISTANCING

As the virus spread, governments around the world asked their citizens to social distance. This meant people should avoid large groups. They should also stay several feet apart.

On March 16, US president Donald Trump asked Americans to socially distance and limit travel. Many state governments took additional steps. They closed schools, restaurants, offices, and stores. By the end of March, 94 percent of Americans were under stay-at-home orders.

With US schools closed, students did video and online learning at home.

During stay-at-home orders, many families connected with loved ones outside their homes using video chat.

19

DO YOU HAVE COVID-19?

If you are **infected** with SARS-CoV-2, it can take 2 to 14 days for COVID-19 to appear. The **disease** has many **symptoms**. It affects people differently.

Some people with COVID-19 show no symptoms. Others have many symptoms. These can range from mild to deadly.

Common COVID-19 symptoms include fever, a dry cough, shortness of breath, and tiredness. Others are a loss of taste or smell, sore throat, headache, muscle aches, or chills.

Healthcare workers used nasal swab tests to check if patients had COVID-19.

TREATING COVID-19

COVID-19 is most dangerous in elderly people or those with other medical conditions. However, even young, healthy people can become very sick from the virus. These people need to be treated in a hospital.

Your body may heal from COVID-19 **symptoms** on its own. But if your symptoms are serious or lasting, call your doctor right away.

WHEN TO GO TO THE HOSPITAL

- Bluish lips or face
- Trouble breathing
- Chest pain
- Confusion
- Trouble waking up

If you think you have COVID-19, stay away from friends and family members. This helps them avoid getting sick too.

AT THE HOSPITAL

In late September 2020, the world had more than 33 million cases of COVID-19. And there was no cure. Some people with COVID-19 got so sick that their organs started to fail. These included patients who were otherwise healthy.

Experts were unsure why these COVID-19 cases were so deadly. Some believed these patients' immune systems **overreacted** to the virus. This can cause extreme **inflammation** and lead to organ failure.

Plastic eyewear and disposable gloves and masks help protect healthcare workers from COVID-19.

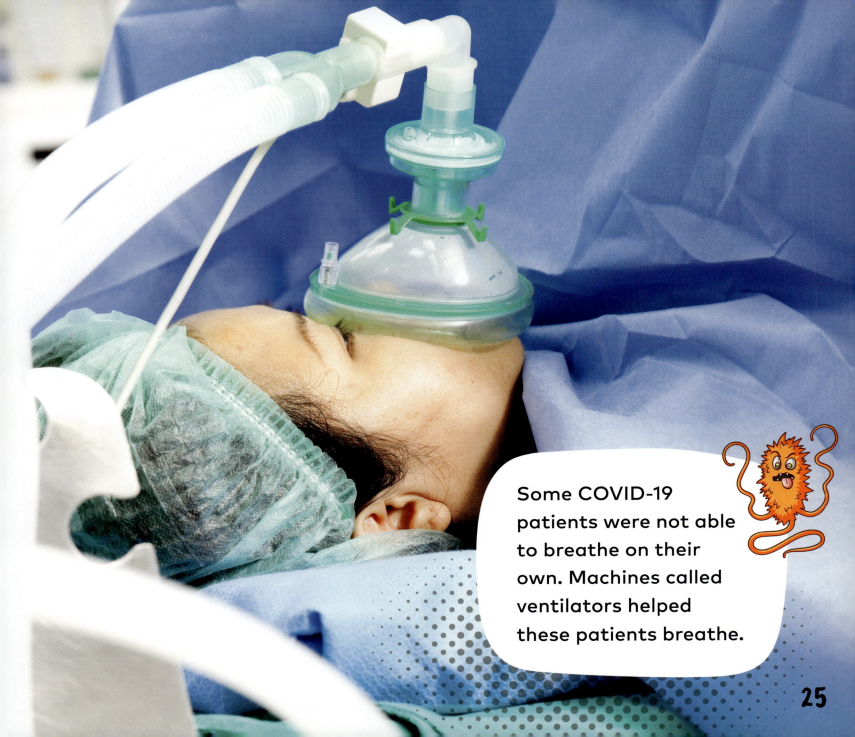

Some COVID-19 patients were not able to breathe on their own. Machines called ventilators helped these patients breathe.

WHAT'S NEXT?

As fall 2020 arrived, the world faced uncertainty. Scientists were working hard to create a COVID-19 **vaccine**. In September, many possible vaccines were being tested. However, none were through trials that would declare them safe for the public.

Health experts said the fastest a COVID-19 vaccine would be ready was 12 to 18 months.

SCIENCE BREAKTHROUGH

A vaccine goes through three stages of testing on people before it is considered safe for the public. During each stage, the vaccine is given to more people. The people are observed for months to make sure the vaccine does not cause harm.

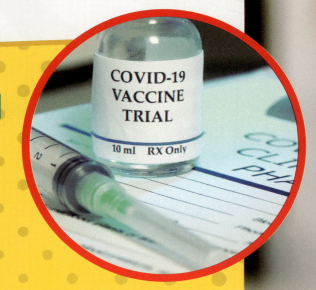

In fall 2020, many schools reopened. However, most US states required students and teachers to wear protective face masks.

PREVENTING COVID-19

The best way to protect yourself from COVID-19 is to stay at home. If you must leave your house, follow these simple rules:

- ☐ Keep at least six feet (2 m) away from people outside your home.
- ☐ Wash your hands often for at least 20 seconds with soap and water.
- ☐ Avoid touching your face.
- ☐ Wear a face mask whenever in public.

COVID-19 can be a dangerous illness. But thanks to your amazing immune system, science, and some healthy habits, your body is ready to face these germ **invaders**!

29

GLOSSARY

coronavirus—any of a family of viruses that are studded with club-shaped spike proteins. These include viruses that cause the diseases MERS, SARS, and COVID-19.

decode—to recognize and interpret into a form people can understand.

detect—to discover or notice.

disease—a sickness.

genetic—of or relating to a branch of biology that deals with inherited features.

infect—to enter and cause disease in. This condition is called an infection.

inflammation—a state of redness, heat, and pain.

invade—to enter and spread with the intent to take over.

mutate—to suddenly change, relating to the genes of a human, a plant, or an animal.

organism—a living thing made up of one or more cells and able to live on its own.

originate—to create or begin.

overreact—to respond to something too strongly.

pandemic—occurring over a wide geographic area and affecting much of the population.

particle—a very small piece of matter, such as an atom or molecule.

release—to set free or let go.

respiratory—having to do with the system of organs involved with breathing.

severe—causing danger, hardship, or pain.

species (SPEE-sheez)—living things that are very much alike.

symptom—a noticeable change in the normal working of the body. A symptom indicates or accompanies disease, sickness, or other malfunction.

vaccine (vak-SEEN)—a substance given through a shot to prevent illness or disease.

ONLINE RESOURCES

To learn more about COVID-19, please visit **abdobooklinks.com** or scan this QR code. These links are routinely monitored and updated to provide the most current information available.

INDEX

animals, 5, 10, 11, 12, 13

bacteria, 5
bats, 12
breathing, 6, 20, 22, 25

China, 10, 12, 13, 17
colds, 8
coronaviruses, 8, 10, 11, 12, 17
coughing, 6, 7, 20

eyewear, 24

fever, 7, 20
fungi, 5

gloves, 24

healthcare workers, 14, 15, 16, 21, 22, 24

influenza, 14

masks, 4, 24, 27, 28

protozoa, 5

replication, 7
respiratory system, 8, 9, 10

SARS-CoV, 11
schools, 18, 27
sneezing, 6, 7
social distancing, 18, 19, 23, 28
spikes, 8
spreading, 4, 6, 7, 12, 14, 15, 16, 17, 18, 24
supplies, 14, 16
symptoms, 16, 20, 22

talking, 6, 7
testing, 16, 21, 26
Trump, Donald, 18

vaccines, 26
ventilators, 25
viruses, 5, 6, 7, 8, 10, 11, 12, 14, 16, 17, 18, 22, 24

wet markets, 13
white blood cells, 7
World Health Organization (WHO), 16, 17